FABULOUS ANIMALS

The Story of the Okapi

Anita Ganeri

capstone

To contact Capstone Global Library please call 800-747-4992, or visit our web site www.mycapstone.com

Edited by Linda Staniford
Designed by Philippa Jenkins
Original illustrations © Capstone Global Library Limited 2016
Picture research by Morgan Walters
Production by Victoria Fitzgerald
Originated by Capstone Global Library Ltd
Printed and bound in China

19 18 17 16 15
10 9 8 7 6 5 4 3 2 1

Library of Congress Cataloging-in-Publication Data
Cataloging-in-publication information is on file with the Library of Congress.
Written by Anita Ganeri
ISBN 978-1-4846-2712-9 (hardcover)
ISBN 978-1-4846-2716-7 (paperback)
ISBN 978-1-4846-2720-4 (eBook PDF)

Acknowledgments
The author and publisher are grateful to the following for permission to reproduce copyright material: Alamy: Melvyn Longhurst, 7, The Natural History Museum, 6, WENN Ltd, 22; American Museum of Natural History: 11, (Lang) left 21; AP Images: APN, 10; Capstone Press: Capstone, (map) 20; Dreamstime: Bonnie Fink, 16, Stu Porter, 8; Glow Images: Juniors Bildarchiv, 15; iStockphoto: Wolfgang_Steiner, 17; Minden Pictures: Sebastian Kennerknecht, 27; National Geographic Creative: RANDY OLSON, 25; Newscom: Jan Philipp Strobel/dpa/picture-alliance, 18, SOUVANT GUILLAUME/SIPA, 19, Tony Kyriacou/REX, 23; Shutterstock: Eric Isselee, 12, 14, Kittibowornphatnon, 5, Tish1, 9; SuperStock: Marka, 26, PhotoAlto, Cover; Wikimedia: Cassell's universal portrait gallery, 5, http://diglib1.amnh.org/articles/chapin, (chapin) right 21, http:/Jami Dwyer, 24, J. Doremus, 13, London Stereoscopic & Photographic Company, 4.

We would like to thank Michael Bright for his invaluable help in the preparation of this book.

007485LEOS16

Contents

Okapi Search 4

A New Animal? 8

Local Knowledge 10

Meet the Okapi 12

Okapi Lifestyle 14

Catching an Okapi 20

In Captivity 22

Okapis Today 24

Okapi Timeline 28

Glossary 30

Find Out More 31

Index 32

Some words are shown in bold, like this. You can find out what they mean by looking in the glossary.

Okapi Search

In the 1880s, a British explorer named Henry Morton Stanley went to the **Congo**, in Central Africa. He heard about a mysterious animal living in the **rain forest**. Local people told him that it looked like a donkey with stripes.

Henry Morton Stanley went on an expedition to Africa.

This is the explorer Harry Johnston.

Stanley told an explorer named Harry Johnston about the animal. Johnston decided to go and search for himself. Some local people helped guide him. They called the animal the "o'api."

On the way to the forest, Johnston met soldiers. They gave him two belts made from striped o'api skin. The belts were used for holding bullets. Johnston sent them back to the London Zoo in England for scientists to study.

These bullet belts are made from o'api skin.

These are o'api skulls.

Johnston himself did not see an o'api. His men got sick and he had to call the expedition off. Later, another soldier gave him a whole o'api skin and two skulls. He sent these back to England, too.

A New Animal?

The scientists were puzzled. They did not know what this new animal was. Could it be a horse, a donkey, or an **antelope**? Some people thought that it was a new type of zebra because of its striped skin.

Zebras also live in Africa.

An okapi's skull is similar to a giraffe's skull.

Then they made an exciting discovery. By studying the skulls that Johnston sent, they figured out that the animal was related to the giraffe. They named it *Okapia johnstoni,* after Johnston. We call it the okapi.

Local Knowledge

Of course, local people knew about okapis long before anyone else had heard of them. Local people hunted okapis for their meat and skin. They caught the okapis in traps and pits.

In the **rain forest** in the **Congo**, local people hunt with nets and spears.

This harp is covered in okapi skin.

For local people, okapis were special animals. They treated okapis with great **respect**. Okapi skins were so precious that only important chiefs were allowed to sit on them.

Meet the Okapi

The okapi is a **mammal** about the size of a horse. It is a similar shape to a giraffe, but it has a much shorter neck and shorter legs.

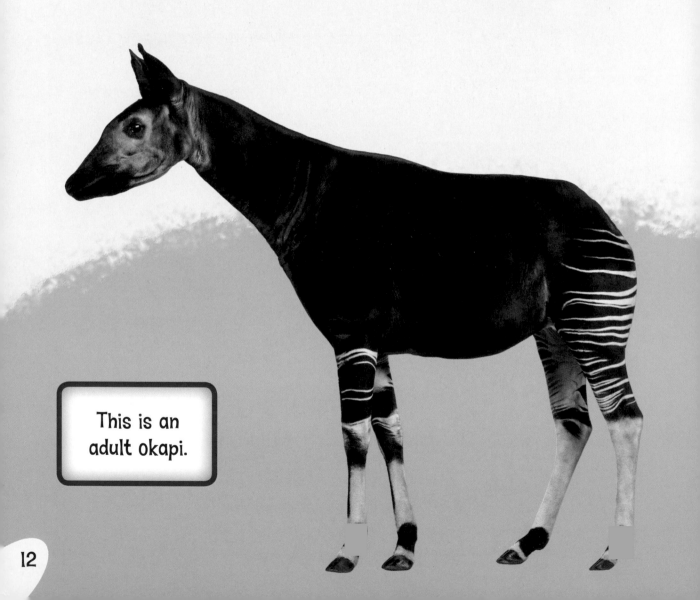

This is an adult okapi.

The Congo rain forest grows along the riverbank.

Wild okapis live in the **rain forest** in the **Congo**, Central Africa. It is always warm in the rain forest. It rains almost every day. Several rivers run through the rain forest.

Okapi Lifestyle

Okapis have reddish-brown fur. They have brown and white stripes on their front and back legs. Their coats are oily so water runs off. This keeps the okapi dry when it rains.

Each okapi has a different pattern of stripes.

Okapis are tricky to spot in the forest.

Okapis are shy animals. It is very difficult to find them in the wild. Their markings help to hide them among the patterns of light and shadow in the forest.

An okapi mostly eats leaves, twigs, and fruit. It pulls them from the trees with its very long tongue. It also uses its tongue to lick its eyelids and ears clean and to **groom** its coat.

An okapi uses its tongue to pull leaves from a tree.

Leopards hunt okapis in the forest.

To find their food, okapis follow paths through the **rain forest**. They use the same paths again and again. As they eat, they listen for leopards and other **predators**.

Usually, okapis live on their own, but mothers and babies stay together. An okapi **calf** can stand up about 30 minutes after it is born. Its mother feeds it with milk.

The mother licks her calf clean.

A mother and calf have similar markings.

Scientists think that the mother's markings help the calf to follow her through the **rain forest**. Calves also make bleating sounds to keep in touch with their mothers.

Catching an Okapi

A lot of what we know about okapis comes from studying them in zoos. But catching a live okapi was not easy. In 1909, an expedition set out from the United States to catch an okapi for the Bronx Zoo in New York.

This map shows the route of the expedition and the area explored.

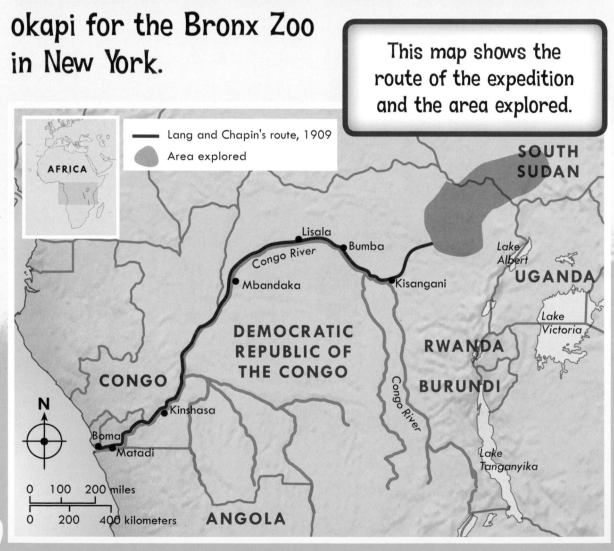

The expedition was led by Herbert Lang (left) and James Chapin.

The men spent months going deeper and deeper into the forest. Finally, they caught a very young okapi **calf**. They fed it **condensed milk**. The milk soon ran out, and the calf died.

In Captivity

The first okapi to live outside Africa was named Buta. She went to Antwerp Zoo in Belgium in 1919 but died after 50 days. In 1937, the first okapi in the United States came to the Bronx Zoo.

This young okapi lives in a zoo.

Keepers take special care of okapis.

Okapis are difficult animals to keep in zoos. They need special care, including very clean living quarters. Early on, many **captive** okapis died. Since then, **keepers** have learned better ways to care for them.

Okapis Today

Today, there are about 10,000 okapis in the wild. They face many dangers. Their **rain forest** home is being destroyed for **timber** and to clear space for farms. Some okapis are killed by **poachers**.

The home of the okapis is being destroyed.

The okapis are guarded by rangers.

In 1992, a large area of the Ituri Rain Forest in the **Congo** was set aside as the Okapi Wildlife **Reserve**. Around 4,000 okapis live there. Specially trained **rangers** and soldiers guard the reserve and the animals.

Scientists are still learning more about okapis. In 2006, a team of **conservationists** made an amazing discovery in the **Congo**. They found the tracks of a new group of okapis in Virunga National Park.

Scientists go on an expedition in Virunga National Park.

A scientist fixes a camera to a tree trunk.

Two years later, scientists from the London Zoo visited the park. They fixed cameras to the tree trunks. They managed to take the first-ever photographs of okapis in the wild.

Okapi Timeline

1890

Henry Morton Stanley mentions okapis in his book about Africa, *In Darkest Africa*.

1899

Stanley meets the explorer Harry Johnston. They discuss the okapi.

1900

Johnston sets out to search for the okapi. He sends two scraps of skin to London, England.

1901

Johnston sends a whole skin and two skulls back to London. The animal is named *Okapia johnstoni*, in his honor.

1909

Herbert Lang and James Chapin lead an expedition to the Congo.

1919

The first okapi to live outside Africa arrives at Antwerp Zoo.

1937

The first okapi in the United States arrives at the Bronx Zoo.

1992

The Okapi Wildlife Reserve is set up in the Congo.

2006

A new group of okapis is discovered in Virunga National Park.

2008

A team from the London Zoo take the first-ever photographs of okapis in the wild.

Glossary

antelope animal that looks like a large deer and runs very fast

calf young okapi

captive animal that lives in a zoo or wildlife park

condensed milk thickened milk with added sugar

Congo country in Central Africa. Its full name is the Democratic Republic of the Congo.

conservationist person who works to protect animals and plants

groom to keep clean; some animals groom each other by picking dirt off each other's fur

keeper person who cares for animals in a zoo

mammal warm-blooded animal that breathes air; mammals have hair or fur; female mammals feed milk to their young

poacher person who hunts or fishes illegally

predator animal that hunts other animals for food

rain forest thick tropical forest where it is hot and rain falls almost every day

ranger person who guards and looks after a wildlife park

reserve land that is protected so that animals may live there safely

respect to believe in the quality and worth of someone or something

timber wood from trees used for building and making things

Find Out More

Books

Ganeri, Anita. *Rainforests* (Explorers). New York: Kingfisher, 2013.

Harris, Tim. *Africa* (Facts at Your Fingertips). Tucson, Ariz.: Brown Bear Books, 2014.

Oxlade, Chris. *Introducing Africa* (Introducing Continents). Chicago: Heinemann Library, 2014.

Websites

FactHound offers a safe, fun way to find Internet sites related to this book. All of the sites on FactHound have been researched by our staff.

Here's all you do:

Visit www.facthound.com
Type in this code: 9781484627129

Index

Bronx Zoo, New York 20, 22

calves 18, 19, 21
catching an okapi 20, 21
Congo, Central Africa 4, 13, 25, 26

food 16, 17

giraffes 9, 12
grooming 16

Ituri Rain Forest 25

keeping okapis in zoos 22, 23

local people 10, 11
London Zoo, England 6

Okapi Wildlife Reserve 25

poachers 24
predators 17

rain forest 4, 13, 15, 19, 24, 25
rangers 25

skin 7, 8, 11
skull 7, 9
Stanley, Henry Morton 4
stripes 4, 6, 8, 14, 15

tongue 16

Virunga National Park 26

wild okapis 24, 27